*Praise for* Memphis

SHORTLISTED FOR THE WATERSTONES
DEBUT FICTION PRIZE

LONGLISTED FOR THE WOMEN'S PRIZE FOR FICTION

'A rhapsodic hymn to Black women' *New York Times Book Review*

'Epic yet intimate' *Cosmopolitan*

'Ferocious and compassionate' *Irish Times*

'An evocative, compelling tale . . . an endearing and unforgettable
cast of characters who find strength in vulnerability, safety in art
and liberation in telling the truth' Robert Jones Jr.

'Black American literature at its finest . . . a symphony of stories'
*Irish Independent*

'A stunning debut . . . this beautifully written, inspiring story is full of
hope and memorable characters' Books of the Year, *Woman and Home*

'A sprawling generational epic and an intimate characters study . . .
incredibly satisfying and deeply affecting' Roxane Gay

'I fell in love with this book and its characters' *Prima*

'Richly impressionistic' *Washington Post*

'Engrossing . . . beautifully written prose, unforgettable characters
and messages of sisterhood and community . . . told from a
captivating Southern female perspective' Best Books of 2022, *NPR*

'This vivid debut novel examines the tragedies, joys and deep
connections of one extraordinary Memphis family' *Booklist*

# Magic Enuff

*Poems*

## Tara M. Stringfellow

JOHN MURRAY

First published in the United States of America in 2024 by Dial Press
First published in Great Britain in 2024 by John Murray (Publishers)

1

Some of the poems in this work originally appeared in the following publications:
*Linden Avenue Literary Journal, Apogee Journal, Jet Fuel Review, Transition,* and *Book Pipeline*

Book design by Susan Turner

A CIP catalogue record for this title is available from the British Library

Hardback ISBN 9781399818377
ebook ISBN 9781399818391

Typeset in Baskerville MT Pro

Printed and bound in Great Britain by Clays Ltd, Elcograf S.p.A.

John Murray policy is to use papers that are natural, renewable and recyclable
products and made from wood grown in sustainable forests. The logging and
manufacturing processes are expected to conform to the environmental regulations
of the country of origin.

Carmelite House
50 Victoria Embankment
London EC4Y 0DZ

www.johnmurraypress.co.uk

John Murray Press, part of Hodder & Stoughton Limited
An Hachette UK company

*For Snoop*
*who is much missed*

*and for Zora*
*who is much loved*

# CONTENTS

We younger Negro artists who create now intend to express our individual dark-skinned selves without fear or shame. If white people are pleased we are glad. If they are not, it doesn't matter. We know we are beautiful. And ugly too. The tom-tom cries and the tom-tom laughs. If colored people are pleased we are glad. If they are not, their displeasure doesn't matter either. We build our temples for tomorrow, strong as we know how, and we stand on top of the mountain, free within ourselves.

—LANGSTON HUGHES,
"The Negro Artist and the Racial Mountain," 1926

In Charleston, I learned about what happens when whiteness goes antic and is removed from a sense of history. It creates tragedies where black grandchildren who have done everything right have to testify in court to the goodness of the character of their slain eighty-seven-year-old grandmother because some unfettered man has taken her life. But I also saw in those families that the ability to stay imaginative, to express grace, a refusal to become like them in the face of horror, is to forever be unbroken. It reminds us that we already know the way out of bondage and into freedom. This is how I will remember those left behind, not just in their grief, their mourning so deep and profound, but also through their refusal to be vanquished. That even when denied justice for generations, in the face of persistent violence, we insist with a quiet knowing that we will prevail.

—RACHEL KAADZI GHANSAH,
"A Most American Terrorist: The Making
of Dylann Roof," *GQ*, 2017

## PICKING

my grandfather
did it
a sack of hemp
tied to his shoulders
filled with clouds
of a fruit inedible
his daddy did it we all did it
we didn't know no betta
he says it was a job
before, it was a life
the only one a Black body
could make a dime on
he trails off
sips the whiskey
I've brought him
you know
being in all dat cotton
I 'member the singing
most of all
a great moan
then 'nother
then 'nother

then 'nother
comin' in waves
startlin'
sorrowful
like the voice
of God

## ORIGINS

Once in Atlantic City, after she couldn't take it any longer, she picked up a bottle and sprayed mustard all over his shirt like silly string. He laughed a high, unsettling laugh in response. Shoved popcorn in his mouth and, walking earshot behind her, said she really must be a no name nigga from Memphis if she think she gon' get anywhere with three babies no degree and a Black face. People on the boardwalk didn't know what to make of it. Some laughed. The women didn't. They looked at her. Then at the stroller.

He gave her a black eye Easter night. She said he was a cheat jus like his Black ass daddy and that's when the fist came—unexpected, quick, soundless. She rebounded against the peach-colored wall. Went after him with a butter knife of all things, circling him round and round the dining room table that was littered with scraps of hours-old pork. The police officer was nicer than most. Let me sit on his lap and play with his flashlight while he took his notes in our kitchen.

My almost-ex-husband is always late. After another fifteen minutes, he walks in whistling a familiar tune, carrying his el-

egance like a satchel and looking as he always did in that cara-
mel wool coat, spitting image of Jack Kennedy. When he sits,
still humming Sinatra, I hiss out an angry whisper: you know
my check engine light has been on for months, I'm at my wit's
end, I'm using this refund for bills. The tax preparer across
from us kindheartedly pretends not to hear him call me a Black
bitch. Years ago we had a pregnancy scare. He fell asleep with
his head on my belly talking about the Cubs and humming
Sinatra songs. *Angels cheer 'cause we're together* he crooned. Over
and over.

Sitting on our back porch in Memphis, I pass my sister the
bottle of rye I've hidden in my purse. Remember when you
damn near killed Tony? she asks. She's talking about the time
I walked into a hotel room in DC and saw my sister, all five
feet ten of her, lying in some foreign origami pose on the floor
while her boyfriend stood over her swaying drunkenly, lei-
surely like paper in the wind. The police officer said I went
after the boy's neck like I was wringing out a damp rag, but I
couldn't tell you what happened. All I remember was Kristen
on the floor and wanting to tear out that boy's trachea with my

own teeth. We laugh about it now. I ask her why on earth she thought it a good idea to date a Yankee. Uppity niggas. The lot of 'em. Her laughter dances along to the song of crickets in the night. Still cracking up she says I looked like a bear bout to claw his eyes out. We sip whiskey. No, I say. I looked like mom.

# HOT COMBS CATFISH CRUMBS AND BAD MEN

lent she'd send us out
*come back with a basketful* she'd call
my sister and i caught black tadpoles
with dark hands thrust into warm bogs
seeking, unafraid
my mother bent over cast iron skillet
read entrails in the hot oil
*men will fail you more than the Lord*
she swung a rosary over the stove
a pendulum pointing south
my sister collected hair thick as a nest
from all the old combs in the house
buried it deep in red clay
*daddycomeback* she chanted

God can stay asleep
these women in my life are magic enuff

## ONLY READ FROM EXODUS
*for Tyre Nichols*

we've cradled enuff bodies of men we love
bleeding out onto uncaring streets
learned to roll my hair with funeral programs
climbed into sheets that may shroud my children
Black rituals. Emmett Till was my Peter Rabbit.
my mama only read from Exodus
*I am the Lord thy God, which have brought thee*
*out of the land of Egypt, out of the house of bondage*

I wonder what most Egyptians thought
when the Jews cried with locusts and plagues
and blood that their lives mattered
my father pulls from a Kool *not a damn thing* he exhales

backing out the drive my mama comes running gasping
you'll need this she says unfolds one long pearl rosary

# TO WHITE FOLK

If I had a son, he would look like Trayvon.
—President Barack Obama


if we can be sisters
you pressin
hot comb to my hair
while Al Green whispers
in Memphis heat
me fussin
tellin you ain't no boy
gonna last as long
as a degree
get yo shit together girl . . .
if we can be that close
so when my children
are being killed
in the streets
you rise up too
you cry into my hair
screaming those were our sons

## THIS WOMAN

my mother
was ten when she got her first black eye
some white man at the counter of a North Memphis
deli fixed her with a square jab that sent her flying
off her stool, ketchup adorning her mother's head
in a blood crown

my mother was inconceivably calm
among the chicken bones on the floor
still as a stone wall
mustard in her hair
while whites screamed at her to go back
to the Memphis zoo
she knelt there on her hands
and knees and tried to breathe
fought the blackness seeping into her vision
the dizziness trying to overtake her
she said she mouthed the Lord's prayer

this woman asks me for anything,
anything at all,
I give it

## BLACK BOYS

*for Adam, my brother*

be rare
when they
be free
be learning
be laughing
be alive
yeah, Black boys
like that
be black pearls
worth the digging

# CONVERSATIONS I NEVER HAD WITH MY FATHER

1.

daddy, would it be betta if I say
something shameful about myself?

I saw you hit mom over and over
and I did nothing but love you

2.

*you should have stayed*
*would've been easier on y'all*
*had I worked it out with mom*

his confession is far too late
as a Marine he should know
he was offering a lit cigarette
to something already long dead

3.

I wish you had taught me weakness
so that I could come home

whimpering, tail between my legs
askin what us got to eat in the fridge
instead, Black man, you raised a warrior
so licking my wounds, I ask for more salt

## FOR TRAYVON'S MOTHER

Ma'am,
I have a brother
same height same build
same fierce fight in him
as your son so every morning
my marrow prays
don't kill this Black son
don't kill this Black son
not *this* one

when white women at the park
spit and yell at him not hurtin a soul,
simply walking his dog
I tell him to say two things:
1: I am an active-duty Airman
and 2: my sister is a lawyer

I was born on a Wednesday, a child of woe,
so I know those words won't stop bullets
but I was also born a poet,
so I know some words can

# THE WHOLE SICK MESS
*for Laquan McDonald*

sitting around a table filled with my kin
my uncle asked why Black kids killing each other
a few blocks away

my auntie hair swept in a silver beehive
shakes her head says
folk crazy nowadays don't have no work ethic

that's when I put my glass of rye down hard
you really think Black kids want to go round shooting
being shot maybe they only in need of opportunity

my daddy claps my back says
she gon be the next Maya Angelou tellin our stories

about how papa couldn't wait to stop pickin cotton
so he enlisted. Went to Germany. Sent a single gold ring
addressed to Early Mae. The two married on VJ day

this is what you need to tell the world about my daddy says
I ask what about the shooting? Police putting bullets in our
  backs?
Tell it all my auntie says. Pullin from a Kool. Tell the whole
  sick mess

JOAN
*for Eric Garner*

I can't prove God but I know you
your breastplate your cropped hair
I imagine you smelled like wild lavender

my mama gave me a pendant
with your face etched in pewter
*don't eva let a man call you crazy*
she said pressing you into my palm

Joan, they are killing Black children
I fear for my very womb where do we go
when a whole country has betrayed us

my mama can't garden, a crime for a Southerner
she crosses herself points to a spot
north purple dark under a magnolia
*look,* she says, *wild lavender grows*

## TO MISS GIANNA FLOYD

I wrote you a Black fairy tale
I understand if you not ready
to read it yet or if your mama
told you to wait a bit and that
just fine this book ain't going
nowhere this book gon be right here
whenever you want it
whenever you get finished playing
outside in that bright beautiful world
your daddy loved so much child,
it's just right to set this aside
Lord knows not a soul on this earth
gon blame you for being out in it—
running laughing breathing

## PHILANDO

I'd cut off my right,
writer's hand gladly
if I never had to eulogize
another poem for
another Black, dead body

I'd put this pen down
maybe take a walk—
it's summatime Chi after all—
maybe pretend to be white
write about trees and binge
drinking and depression
no one would expect
anything but

you are dead and
I am a Black poet

I'd cut off my right,
writer's hand gladly
if I never had to eulogize
another poem for
another Black, dead body

# I DREAMT THE KKK WERE IN MY LIVING ROOM

and I had made everyone lemonade
they sipped, offered pleasantries
my house, the antiques
how could they see I asked
with only those tiny slits
for eyes and we all laughed

after a bit, it got quiet
so I broke the silence with
what I thought my mom
and my grandma and hers
would've wanted me to say—

I poisoned y'all lemonade

## DEAR TUPAC

I remember my mother pulling the car over
when K97 announced your death
she pulled into an empty Blockbuster
parking lot turned the car off
put her head on the wheel
and asked in a whisper
who would honor us now

I had no answer I was eleven
and you were the only man in my house
my mother got the record player in the divorce
fought for it like Ali in the ring
touching the sides of the vinyl
like a hot plate of chkndumplins in her hands
she would place you down
gentler than any of her children
align needle to groove
and when *I ain't mad at cha* came on
or *dear mama*
she'd hang her head
not even dance

not even mouth along to the words
*he's our prophet* she'd say over and over

in 1996, no one had ever called my mother
anything other than a welfare queen
you made her feel like just that last word
no one ever told her to keep her head up
no one ever told her when a no name nigga
says you you ain't nothin' don't believe him
and if he can't learn to love you you should leave him
these words were almost foreign to her

so I'm tellin you
when you died
our still car in that empty parking lot
my mother's forehead on that steering wheel
shaking back and forth in disbelief
I was only eleven
I had no idea the world could end that quietly

## TO KANYE

my mother told us
that if we eva got lost
in a store or on our bikes a mile from home
find the nearest Black woman
and stay there

Black women are outposts of sanity
or safety
my mother didn't differentiate between the two
go to her she'd say
and stay your Black ass put till I come get you
Her becoming the collective pronoun, the womb for us all
as if this Her could shine a beacon into the sky
only Black mothers could see

now that I am woman
I know there was some truth
in her command:
Kanye
I need you
to lay your head here
right here and tell me what ails you

or sleep
or cry
but stay here
at home atop a Black breast
the only thing in this world
I know that's strong enuff to save it

# FOR HARRIET

"I grew up like a neglected weed—
ignorant of liberty, having
no experience of it."

what you did with two brown hands
and not a civil right to your name
armies heralded in gold and bronze
could not have done more
and haven't

*hail mary* is simply a poem
for a woman poor, alone
who had a son no one believed in
what Black woman hasn't lived this?
where are our psalms?

but you
mile by mile
sojourning across Smokies
and Appalachia thirteen times
what you did with two brown hands
cannot be explained

you see, even a century or two later

this world still needs proof

a Black woman

is the strongest compound

God could ever forge

ON WITNESSING A STABBING
IN OVERTON PARK, MEMPHIS, TN
CHRISTMAS DAY

what I'll remember most is that
when I ran that mile
screaming for help
to call the police
to save the elderly man
being stabbed senselessly repeatedly

is that my city listened to this Black woman
I must have been a sight
the white jogger in the neon shirt
ran and tackled the guy
still armed with the knife
and a white lady took ahold
of my hound's leash in one hand
called the police with her other

they rose up like members of my own family
like so many Marines and Airmen
miracles all around: no one died that day
and them white folk believed me

ME, RECEIVING MY FIRST PERIOD

MEMPHIS, TENNESSEE

men call it our curse
she says shaking her halo
but it is not a sin
to bleed for the world

she points at my opening

this is not of God
this is what we women
have created

this is called brave
this is called love

my mother coos
as she dampens a rag
presses it between
my thighs

# MY MOTHER, RECEIVING HER LAST PERIOD

Memphis, Tennessee

my mother crouched
with cupped hands,
felt in her brownness
for that familiar peat,
wet clumped earth
after tornado
and felt nothing

so she wandered for it
how as a child lost
I'd search for her
in a grocery store,
willed it with walking
hungered for it,
then realized those pains
were only of hunger
so she sat
at our kitchen table
and ate cold,
buttered potatoes

it came once more

without reason

on a day not circled in red

on the refrigerator calendar

like a daughter who rarely visits

and when she does

it is both shame and joy

she knew then

when it had finally gone

how she had loved

even the pain

# THAT ONE TIME MY COLLEGE BOYFRIEND HIT ME

the wind knocked out of me,
I took a knee on the movie theater floor
and I thought about Nefertiti
bowing at the cusp of her own altar
built in her own image
the most beautiful woman alive
a face that could launch a fleet
who only knelt at her own statues
and if a thousand years passed
archaeologists would find me still
kneeling, face upturned toward
this white boy in stunned silence

reading my entrails
a mystic would say
that I was woman
and Black
and wanted too much

# I COULDN'T FIND THIS IN THE BIBLE

but I reckon that when Eve
cast out of Eden
her children cursed
her husband rendered mute
I bet she came to love the blood
more than her ravenous children
more than her docile unhusband
married in the incest of creation
without a thought of his own

and if Eve is a curse
if it is a sin to want
for more than play
in some meaningless jungle
then God was never a woman
and although Everything,
lacks so very much
for it is no curse
to bleed for the sins of man

this is called brave
this is called love

## DREAMS

Early Mae hooked up to a dialysis machine
wheezing at times told me I was a fool to trust
white men, Black men
said walk alone head up crawl if I must
my grandmother was an oracle

I dream of pale riders and towers falling
brown women rounded up in droves like horses
wake up talking in tongues
the man in my bed says I worry too much
I flinch when he touches me—
Black women must, Black women must

I dream of Ghana waking up under baobab
djembe drums—a Black heartbeat
villagers with brown hands in my hair
demanding a poem when I open my mouth
a thousand cranes fly out

I dream of a daughter, never a husband
perhaps, I, too, am an oracle

# A POEM FOR BLACK GIRLS IN THEIR TWENTIES

join this ritual
learn to make greens
learn to strip
stem after green stem
clean leaf after leaf
the dead, wet flies

cook the collards for hours
boiling with pigs' feet
sing while you do this

catch the pitch
of your mother's voice
comb your sister's hair

use the best plates
taste how delicious
how enduring

this is what we made
when they chained us

together like dogs
in a savage new world
and bid us toil

no, we said
we will sing

POEM AT 30

*for Sonia Sanchez*

always ferocious
skinny wild
as some dark thing
God never named
bringing clay turtles snakes
into the house
slipping out from grips
laughing at my mother's shrieks
my father insists
to this day
no man can tame me
please cheer with me
for he is right he is right

# POEM AT 35

it is a lonely admission:
that God is the only man
who's stayed
that most nights
I wrap myself with words
and fur and sit by a low fire
and think how they talk
even my family—
spinster. siren. serpent.

yes, I have fangs

this Black woman
back bent over dying fire
has learned to sharpen
necessary tools

# NOLA VS. MEMPHIS

my stepmom stalked
leopard-like across this new house
not mine I was told and told
but there she was
splendid in her Kenyan house dresses
cooking étouffée and mirliton
declaring over Easter lamb
a pointed, telling boast
that her family were never slaves

she, all gold skin and red nails
I, nappy hair and dirty Converse
hidden behind some novel

I guess she loved me best she could
this dark, this defiant thing
descended from nothing but cotton
and cornbread
who distrusted her food
who refused to call her anything other
than her first, government name
who flashed teeth and tomboy curses
*one day Imma write bout you*

the other day I saw a flock of birds
out my window not diving for food
not seeking shelter
just dancing in the wind
sparrows flying just to soar

maybe the fight in me is gone
maybe I should grab your hand
maybe we should soar into the kitchen
tell my father we love him

## KRISTEN

I should've put down the books and followed you
caught more tadpoles
told more lies
bitten more innocent children

it's not an easy thing to know
I am a better poet than sister

and becoming that took time, time away from you

but I'll say this here
because you may not know it
may doubt it because I never showed it enuff
but I'd walk across hot coals for you
and if magic didn't exist, I'd create it

# ON CONTEMPLATING LEAVING MY WHITE HUSBAND

1.

in my grandmother's kitchen
counter covered with chopped onions
she stood over cutting board
and asked why on earth
did I think that white boy
would be any different
from the lot of them

when I didn't answer
she handed me an onion to peel
said I had work to do
and I must do it alone


2.

I inherited distrust from my mama
she hers and so on
do not fault us
we have buried hair in red clay
praying for men to come back to us
fingers blood red nails dirty
chanting *daddyvisitdaddyvisitdaddy*

3.

I am Black, southern, lost in Chicago
you were no refuge
grabbed my arm hard when the woman in Lincoln Park
called me the word we all knew was coming
and you
you were the one who led me home
you were the one who steered me like cattle


4.

suppertime would be the hardest
I'd break down touching onions
palming them remembering


5.

if we had a son
you with him in the store
the manager not believing
me away on business
what would you do then

what would you do then
what would you do then


6.


my grandma says
if you bury sumpthin of a man's
a comb works best
he's yours forever


7.


I dug a hole in dark Illinois earth
a quiet spot by the lake
and as I covered dirt
over the ring I never liked anyway
I sang
I sang all the gospel songs I knew

## MY EX-HUSBAND

loved me but in white
I spoke only negro
meaning I did not know fairy tale
saw it in movies, yes, but saw my daddy
spit on in a park in Chicago
Grimms negated

I can't speak white
though I tried lord knows
pressed brown hands to pale fingers
in some sign language morse code
palms screaming
dontchu remember Africa?
why you treat your sistah?

Forgive me
my granddaddy was strung up
on a poplar on Poplar Avenue in Memphis
hanging there for weeks
all cause he applied for the police academy . . .

my love, I should've warned:
a Black woman is no picnic

SUNDAYS

in my kitchen
missing the microwave my ex-husband took
I stand over sink cleaning chitlins for hours
and wonder if a white body can really love
a Black one

mama says no
says I shoulda known betta runnin round Chicago
she don't know why I came to live amongst northerners—
ogres who devour decent women
and left her baby alone in a half empty apartment
cryin over a white man

on Sundays my mama would press velvet gloves
into my tiny hands and whisper
that I betta not act a fool in front of all these nice white folk
handed me a butterscotch
pointed her lace gloved finger at Matthew 10:29:
*not one sparrow can fall to the ground*
*without your Father knowing it*

my husband hated the smell of chitlins
even when I boiled them with potatoes

and opened all the windows
cook them when I'm gone he'd say

when she hears my crying on the other end
my mama sighs and says God is everywhere
Mary just lit a fire in the stove
Ruth went out to pick greens
they all eatin chitlins
I shoulda neva trusted a man
don't eat God's work
don't see our hand in it
don't ask if he can say grace

# IN YO LIFE

I was eight when my mother filled with rage and Jameson
crunched a love letter she found from my father's secretary
in his suit pocket and came at me in her delirium,
holding the pulp of paper like a warm heart in her hand
and through tears sobbed
*don't chu eva*—held up the pulsing letter
*do this to anutha woman eva in yo life*

she stumbled away defeated as Job,
lost as Joseph and left me for more liquor
I was thirty when I left my husband
to be with no one in particular
which is much worse my mother screamed
for the life of her she could not understand
why God bid her raise a selfish child

don't pay mama no mind my sister says
sometimes you need a sister like a sailor needs a compass

mama prolly still achin over daddy
aren't we all I ask

## THE DAY OF MY DIVORCE

I never told a soul
but later that night
amid all his boxes
I danced, I danced


. . . and all the music was Black

## MARY, DID YOU HAVE A CHOICE?

my mother didn't
she packed all our things my brother in her womb
*it's ok baby* she cooed hand on extended belly
fled in the night with her children
born and unborn. poor Black beaten screaming into
motel room pillows God you an angry God
my knees are rug burnt from the love of You

I wonder if the Lord ever asked you
woman. warrior. mother to Joan of arc & Harriet
the only true prophets I've known
what you wanted

I see you now, shaking your curls
remembering your hand on your belly
with each sharp step of the donkey
searching the stars in a dark desert night
for a sign knowing only this truth—

*if He wants a savior, this baby better be a girl*

# LOVE HAIKU

1.

it takes all of me
even atop other men
not to scream your name

2.

people hold no worth
they are mere decorations
to string in your hair

3.

this will end. all things
must. I rejoice in your voice
echoing poems

4.

I am pale pink crane
you—rippling blue lotus pond
I thirst none but you

5.

without you, my friend,
is Loneliness. she, at least,
hears my heart splinter

6.

I await your next
text how I waited as a
girl for my first blood

7.

the moment you said
I need you, my pulse opened
and out poured rubies

8.

that wife of yours best
worship your every touch
because I cannot

9.

I want to show you
me all spread out like laundry
naked, bare, waiting

10.

o, I have been hurt
whipped donkey carryin' rice
uphill, deserted

11.

why do we hurt each
other? are we afraid of
souls swirling like paint?

12.

friend, concerned, at brunch:
girl, you look a damn mess. jus'
tell him you love him

IN MY GODMOTHER'S GARDEN
*for Lucille Clifton and Sonia Sanchez*

we picked
the roses
red
yellow
she held them gingerly
in her gloved fist
shaded by magnolias
we dug in red southern clay
for anything salvageable
bursting
ready

Black men, who will pick me
this wild
yellow thing
if you do not?

## PICKING NO. 2

she would send us out
knobbed manicured hand
pointing west
my grandmother knew
every blackberry bush
in Memphis
would taste and pinch
picking out the perfect ones
showing my sister and I
how to taste for imperfection
you were just as dark
tart like the discarded blackberries
elaborate as the cobbler
complicated crisscross of crisp
and crushing correctness
I told myself don't discard this one
taste all of him
your favorite color is powder blue
so was my father's Mustang
nestled as close as possible
to a Virginia blackberry bush
he set me on the hood

pointed out the ripe black ones
like constellations
I suppose I loved you even then
forming my first memory
tiny feet on the hood
reaching for blackness.
reaching for you
coming up just short

## WE ARE ACCUSED

of reliving memories
replicating moments
that were miraculous
the first time
I heard you snore
in a cloudless Chicago night
as dark as your skin . . .
we do it again and again
hurling ourselves towards each other
perfecting
savoring
a synthesis repeated
if it had sound,
how we would echo

## AGONY

is not beautiful
or poetic
my very sinews and pulse
ache from beating
constant
thoughts of you
it is not romantic
to see a Black woman
crumble up
fold in on herself
like a dead spider

## A SONNET

last summer
when you called
tellin' me y'all
were having a girl
I struggled, but
managed to climb
up the highest shelf
in my Virginia kitchen
lifted my daddy's
last bottle of bourbon
and late into the night
let Al Green explain
to me that loving a man
means letting him go

DINNER PREP

you burnt the rice
your face said it all
the lowered eyes
the long sigh
you had no idea
the many times
I had burned *Nishiki*
and there was no one
to lift my chin or
cup my face as if to say
darling, how you've fed
this stumbling, this hungry heart

POEM AT MIDNIGHT
*for Sonia Sanchez*

tonight
I asked God
what to do about you
in the waiting silence
pregnant, expectant
long as the years
I've longed for you
I suddenly saw myself
clear as day
naked, treading water
swimming in some ancient sea
same color as your eyes

God's like that
sending messages
you can't quite figure
sink or swim sink or swim
exasperated,
knees numb from kneeling
this Black woman rose up
then I swore God an oath:

that when it is built,
my house in his heart,
no other woman will dare enter

# TIRED BLACK WOMAN

find another you say
like I have not found men
who broke everything:
doors. mirrors. once,
a left rib, tender for months

don't wait for me you say
I have this whole other world
filled with strollers and baby
bottles and love I will not give you
like I do not know the rules
geishas come through the back door

go on now you say, out into that world
ain't you brave? ain't you a goddess?
like evenings I do not listen to the birds
until even they stop their song
like I've never torn this house apart
searching for my sword and shield

# I DON'T KNOW WHY

people
on the bus never rise
for the old or for the Black women
with kids
why people never write
letters anymore
why I found a brush
on your nightstand
with hair as long as mine
but not my color
not as thick
not as curly
not Negro
I know why people lie
truths can be as naked
as bone
as singular
as me in our bed
wondering if you call
the other woman
darling

FOR MY EX

1.

so it has come
to the measuring
of broken hearts
smoking menthols
over the ashes of us

what glory
how we turned fire
how we took raw earth
made it blossom
sunflowers planted
before I left

yes, I did leave
and while you turned
to drink to drug to pussy
not mine
I wrote this poem for you

2.

you once said
I'm not the best
you've ever had

then you know nothing
of mountains
of a stiff brown body
standing before the world
naked
fierce
declaring
that everything on earth
has tried to diminish me
and has failed

if there is something wilder
than me
stronger than me
fiercer
better
God's still building it

3.

I told you my favorite animal
don't be prey you said
grabbing a chunk of my hair
twisting back my neck
kissing me there
breathing heavy into my ear
*gazelle*—I only like
how it sounds

maybe.

maybe this Black woman
is tired
is lonely
doesn't mind the sound at all
of waiting in warm, tall grass
of waiting to be plucked
by some wild, brown thing . . .

4.

I keep a cigarette you rolled me
in the small of my purse
finger it and wonder
what else your hands are doing
what mango are they palming
what woman are they inside
I wonder what god did I smite
what sin did I not kneel out
what wrong have I done
that my brown hands failed
to hold on to you


5.

I survived you
as I have soldiered thru
other, harder things
my father leaving
my mother's disdain
my rape

too young to know
it was so much more
than pain
and darkness
and hardwood floor
and wire hanger
but here I am
*y mira, cómo bonita*
I write this in Cuba
down to my last cuc
a little drunk
off the mojitos and the men
countless as the mosquitoes . . .

in the monumental
loss of you
I've learned
to fully know
my birthright:

behold:
the year of the ox

# A BLACK WOMAN'S HEART

my mother
is a fixer of hearts
a cardiac nurse
every night
during the rounds
she holds them
right in her hands
palms the organs with
the grace, the dignity
of a communion wafer
so she's the one I call
gasping, choking out
what you did,
what I said
in the background
there's a faint beep
of a heart monitor
then a sigh as long
as any rosary

a Black woman's heart?

a beat of silence

daughter, I don't know
of a stronger muscle

MAYBE

it's the poet in me
I remember my father
tucking me in
reading me Byron
proclaiming in a voice
soaked with whiskey—
go
go get your Nobel

maybe
it's the Southerner in me
a long history of women
sitting at windowsills
waiting for men
who'll never show

or maybe
(and this is what I pray)
it's the woman in me
(tiny. Black. *peligrosa*)
who speaks broken Spanish
who buys you croissants

watches you eat them
naked in my kitchen
savoring every stolen second
maybe she's the reason
one single command
pounds in my aorta
like a djembe drum—

go
go get him

ROUTE TO FREEDOM

our last date you mentioned
that no matter the girl
no matter how in love
best believe you have
an exit plan
an escape hatch
a Rita Hayworth poster
hiding your route to freedom

when I was six
I packed a bag
sheets. an umbrella. Barbies.
nonsense really yet I was convinced
that I could jump from our 13th-story
Okinawan penthouse and parachute
down to the earth unscathed

Lord knows what stopped me
the height perhaps
or the rush of tropical wind
from the open window
shrugging the pack from my shoulders

perhaps I knew even then
that some things were worth
staying for, sticking out
that life doesn't come with
escape hatches
especially for lil Black girls

perhaps I knew even then
that I had work to do
poems to write
you to meet

## TO THE CYNIC

outside my building,
a tiny brown bird
has crashed into a window
and now rests at my feet
cinnamon tufts of feather
lie in an ignorant mass
and yet . . .

the one wing left
stretched outward, upward,
resembling something like a fist,
resembling something like triumph

## ACKNOWLEDGMENTS

The fact that I am a Black woman writing poetry in a coun-
try where once upon a time I would have had my hand cut off
for simply holding a book is not lost upon me. Most mornings,
when I sit down to write with my cappuccino and my cigarette,
I stare out my window overlooking honeysuckle and wisteria
and often, I think about Phillis Wheatley. I think about the fact
that she could write in perfect iambic pentameter, a feat for any
poet, a small miracle knowing she wrote at the age of thirteen.
And although she was proof of slavery's moral ineptitude—the
world knew damn well that it was a crime to enslave a girl des-
tined to be better than Byron—no American press was willing
to publish a collection of her poetry. She turned to England,
where her poetry was not only published but heralded. Still,
despite the fact she was a literary genius, despite the fact she
had been sold to a family when she was only about six or seven,
her age guessed since her baby teeth were still falling out upon

her sale, the family who owned her did not free her. Nor did the American public warm to her. For that would have meant acknowledging a Black woman's intelligence, creativity, dignity. That would have meant having a frank conversation about the hypocrisy and evils of slavery. That would have meant reading literature written by someone American society deemed problematic and, thus, chose to ignore.

The shameful erasure of Black women in American literature is still happening in my state of Tennessee, which has banned classic and necessary books by Toni Morrison, Angie Thomas, and Alice Walker, among others. When I was a teacher in the Shelby County School system back in 2017, there was not a single author of color taught on the tenth-grade curriculum. For the entire year. Because I am an American and the descendant of slaves forced into centuries of illiteracy, I taught them anyway. For National Poetry Month in April, my class read poems by Sonia Sanchez and Claudia Rankine and, of course, Phillis Wheatley. I brought in a portable record player my dad got me for my thirtieth birthday, and we listened to Ma Rainey and Bessie Smith records, to the same songs mentioned in *The Color Purple*, for I was determined to teach that banned book to my Memphis students at White Station High School, so help me God, if it was the last thing I would do. For my class on theme, my students and I planted purple kale and African violets in the school garden so we could look out our window and stop and take notice of the color purple growing wild in a field much like God and Walker would've wanted us to do. I felt it my duty as an English literature teacher to do just that—teach English literature. Which meant teaching Homer as well as Langston Hughes, making certain my students knew Lucille Clifton as well as they knew Emily Dickinson, instilling a respect for both the Enlightenment and the Black Arts Movement in my classroom. I, like so many Southern teachers, dabbled in criminality for teaching content written by the greatest American writers in our Western canon, who just so happened to be Black. Who just so happened to be women. And for that, I knew I could be prosecuted, persecuted, and, perhaps, assassinated.

Not a soul on this earth can dissuade me from the belief, the fact, that there is a correlation between state policies banning African American literature in libraries and schools and the growing wave of nationalistic violence my peoples are suffering at the hands of mad gunmen prescribed to the notion that Black folk are subhuman. Worth killing. Certainly not worth reading. I also believe and know in my Black, Southern bones that this country has a long, sordid history of keeping books out of the hands of my people. A tactic by oppressors to keep a people silenced, without agency, enslaved in perpetuity. Will we continue to let the voices of Black writers go unread simply because the content makes us uncomfortable? But isn't that the point of a good book? To make the reader uncomfortable? To force the reader to ask higher questions of themselves and their place and role in humanity? To ask ourselves if we are doing enough? And are we any good? Who would've thought that the front lines of our next great American war would be American libraries? So most mornings, I sit with my coffee and wonder what Wheatley would've thought about a crazed gunman walking into a church in Charleston or a dollar store in Florida and killing every Black person at hand. I reckon as a former slave she'd think not much has changed in this country. That two hundred and fifty some odd years after Wheatley's first poem was published, here we are as Black poets declaring in a voice made weak by time and fate, but strong in will, that our lives matter.

Still, I have hope. Perhaps because I am a poet, perhaps because I was made in the South, perhaps because of the Catholic in me, I am used to faith. And perhaps because I am the daughter of a Marine, the sister of an Airman, the granddaughter of a World War II war hero, I have faith, too, in this country. Which means I have love for her. An indescribable, overwhelming love. Felt whenever Sha'Carri Richardson wins a race, or whenever Beyoncé hits a high note, or whenever a student of mine reads Nikki Giovanni out loud. It is a love evidenced by my publisher, Dial Press, and my incredible editors, Katy Nishimoto and Whitney Frick, who believe as fervently as I do that a Black woman sitting down to write a sonnet is a gorgeous and courageous act. I'd like to also give thanks to Sabrena Khadija, once again, for the beautiful cover, and to my team at Dial—Brianna Kusilek, Corina Diez, Maya Millett, Michelle Jasmine, Debbie Aroff, Rose Fox, Avideh Bashirrad, Robert Siek, Angela McNally, Susan Turner, Donna Cheng, and Christina Johnson—for everything they've done and do for me.

I have hope because Soumeya Bendimerad Roberts, my agent at HG Literary, took a chance on me seven years ago when I had twenty pages of my debut novel *Memphis* written and not much else other than sheer will and a dream to finish a great American novel. Since then, she has championed me into the writer I am today. This poetry collection would not exist without Soumeya, who sent me a rather furtive and conspiratorial one-line email one morning in 2022 *that wasn't it high time to show the world some of my poetry.* What a force. What a blessing I have in my life.

I have hope because I know that my family has done nothing but make this country great since my ancestors arrived in chains. And my family must know that I would move mountains for them. But in case they need it in print: my mother, my father, my sisters and brothers, my new niece, Zora; my uncles and aunties, cousins and kin—all of you make my life delicious and meaningful. And no amount of success or fame or books sold or parties attended or speeches given mean a lick as much as when my mom kisses my forehead or my father claps my knee and tells me that I'm one hell of a daughter. Next time we meet, let's pour one out for Papa and Snoop and Auntie Joyce. How I miss them.

And finally, I have hope because folk in this country took one look at this tiny Black girl reciting Byron and Countee Cullen and knew, just knew, that all I needed was paper and a pen. From Mr. Thomas Cook, my tenth-grade English teacher at Craigmont High School in Memphis, Tennessee, who taught me iambic pentameter, like Wheatley, when I was only thirteen, to Ruth Lilly Poet Laureate Ed Roberson, who labored with me over these lines early Saturday mornings at the Harold Washington Library in Chicago for hours until he pointed at my page and said, "There. You've made magic there. Now make more." From Naliaka Wakhisi, dear friend, who gave me a spot on Northwestern's Black poetry open mic, Africafé, to Elizabeth Sampson with the Chicago Poetry Center, and to everyone at Women & Children First bookstore in Chicago, who gave me my first grand opening. And to my father, a fellow poet, who taught me an invaluable, revolutionary lesson: to love poetry. How I do.

We are living in some troubled times in this country. We

live in a time where we go a week without a mass shooting and we call that a triumph. We live in a time in which we'd give a teacher a 9mm handgun to defend her classroom rather than a copy of *The Color Purple*. We live in a time in which Black children are gunned down for simply knocking on someone's door, for listening to music, or for walking home. We live in a time in which previous generations had more reproductive say-so over their bodies than I do. And yet, I believe in the power of a poem to reshape nations. Wheatley did it. Two hundred and fifty some odd years ago. At thirteen. So every morning, with my coffee and with my worried thoughts, I write. Despite the chaos, and the senseless violence, I write. And in every poem, every tender word, there is a prayer that this country will finally see me and mine as beautiful and be ashamed. For we have sung the song of America quite beautifully for quite some time. And we ain't goin' nowhere.

—*The Author*